Voices of

WORLD WAR I

STORIES FROM THE TRENCHES

by Ann Heinrichs

Consultant:
Eli Paul
Vice President of Museum Programs
National World War I Museum
Kansas City, Missouri

CAPSTONE PRESS
a capstone imprint

Edge Books are published by Capstone Press,
151 Good Counsel Drive, P.O. Box 669, Mankato, Minnesota 56002.
www.capstonepub.com

Books published by Capstone Press are manufactured with paper
containing at least 10 percent post-consumer waste.

Library of Congress Cataloging-in-Publication Data
Heinrichs, Ann.
  Voices of World War I : stories from the trenches / by Ann Heinrichs.
    p. cm. — (Edge books. Voices of War)
  Includes bibliographical references and index.
  Summary: "Describes first-hand accounts of World War I from those
    who lived through it"—Provided by publisher.
  ISBN 978-1-4296-4737-3 (library binding)
  ISBN 978-1-4296-5626-9 (paperback)
  1. World War, 1914–1918—Juvenile literature. I. Title. II. Series.
  D522.7.H456 2011
  940.4'8—dc22   2010000995

Editorial Credits
Kathryn Clay, editor; Tracy Davies, designer; Svetlana Zhurkin,
    media researcher; Laura Manthe, production specialist

Photo Credits
akg-images/ullstein bild, 9; Alamy/Classic Image, 19; Corbis/Bettmann, 17, 25;
Corbis/Underwood & Underwood, 13; DVIC/NARA, cover (top), 6, 22 (bottom);
From "Over the Top" by Arthur Guy Empey, published in 1917, 18; Getty Images/
Cincinnati Museum Center/Felix Koch, 26 (top); Getty Images/George Eastman
House/Castelnau, 15; Getty Images/Hulton Archive, 7, 26–27; Getty Images/
Popperfoto, 21, 23; Getty Images/Slava Katamidze Collection, 11; Getty Images/
Topical Press Agency, 22 (top); iStockphoto/Linda Steward (letter), cover; Library
of Congress, 14; Map Resources, 5 (inset); Mary Evans Picture Library, 10;
Shutterstock/Adam Tinney (flames), cover, back cover, 1; Shutterstock/Ann Triling
(stars), throughout; Shutterstock/Benjamin Haas (barb wire and smoke), cover, back
cover, 1; Shutterstock/Bob Orsillo (airplane), cover; Shutterstock/Cagri Oner (torn
paper), throughout; Shutterstock/Igorsky (stone wall), 17, 21, 24; Shutterstock/
Katarzyna Mazurowska, 28; Shutterstock/kzww (rusty background), throughout;
Shutterstock/Lora Liu (paper background), throughout; XNR Productions (map), 5

Printed in the United States of America in Stevens Point, Wisconsin.
042011   006196R

TABLE OF CONTENTS

1 THE WAR TO END ALL WARS

Archduke Franz Ferdinand of Austria-Hungary rode through Sarajevo on a sunny June day in 1914. Suddenly a gunman sprang from a side street. He pointed a pistol into the car and fired, killing the archduke and his wife. The shooter was a Bosnian Serb. He wanted all Serbs to form an independent nation.

The archduke's death paved the way for World War I. Austria-Hungary first declared war on Serbia. Russia joined Serbia's side. Germany declared war on Russia and France and invaded Belgium. In defense of Belgium, Great Britain declared war on Germany.

The warring nations formed two opposing sides. Germany and Austria-Hungary were the major **Central powers**. The **Allied powers** included Great Britain, France, Belgium, Russia, and later the United States. The United States joined the war in 1917 after German submarines began attacking U.S. ships.

Bloody battles raged on land, at sea, and in the air. Some called it the Great War. Others called it the war to end all wars.

From 1914 to 1918, millions of people from around the world fought in World War I. Survivors came away with stories of unspeakable terror and uncommon courage. You're about to learn the details from a few of these brave fighters.

Central powers: a group of countries that fought the Allied powers in World War I; the Central powers included Germany and Austria-Hungary

Major Allied and Central Powers

Allied powers: a group of countries that fought the Central powers in World War I; the Allies included the United States, Great Britain, France, Russia, and Italy

2 CAPTAIN EDDIE RICKENBACKER: AMERICA'S ACE PILOT

Air warfare was new in World War I. Fighter pilots were known for being daring, fearless flyers. Captain Eddie Rickenbacker was America's top army pilot in the war. He shot down 26 German planes. That record earned him the nickname "America's **Ace** of Aces."

RACE CAR DRIVER

Eddie Rickenbacker loved speed. He was a champion race car driver. He also designed car engines. When war broke out, Rickenbacker knew he wanted to race through the skies. "Aviation had always been a mystery as well as a delight to me," he said.

ace: someone who has shot down at least five enemy aircraft

Rickenbacker's dreams would soon come true. He joined the army in 1917 and was shipped off to France. There he took flight training and learned to shoot down planes. He joined a group of American flyers in the Hat-in-the-Ring Squadron. It was the first squadron of U.S. fighter pilots to fly over enemy lines.

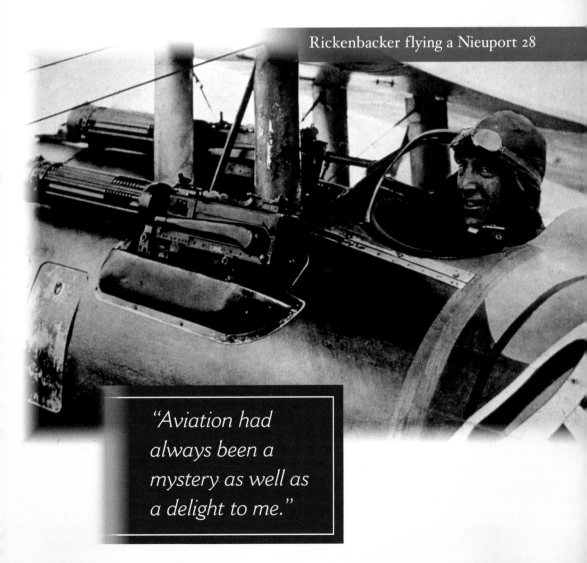

Rickenbacker flying a Nieuport 28

"Aviation had always been a mystery as well as a delight to me."

HIT BY ENEMY FIRE!

Rickenbacker and the other pilots spent their days making test flights and checking their equipment. They tried on their outfits too. High-altitude pilots wore "teddy bear suits." These warm, padded outfits kept the pilots warm when flying in the cold air.

Soon Rickenbacker had his first mission over enemy territory. The idea of his first trip was both scary and exciting. He suited up quickly and was ready to go. "It takes about ten seconds to step into your teddy bear suit, slip a flying helmet over your head and snap on the glasses," he said.

As he soared across enemy lines for the first time, Rickenbacker suddenly felt ill from nerves. But an explosion behind him meant he had little time to think about being sick. His plane had been hit by enemy fire! Black puffs of smoke trailed from the rear of his plane. **Shrapnel** from exploding shells tore through the tail. But Rickenbacker managed to keep control of his aircraft and landed safely.

shrapnel: small pieces of metal scattered by an exploding shell or bomb

Back on the ground, Rickenbacker examined the damage to his plane. He saw that shrapnel had come within a foot of his body. He turned pale when he realized how close he'd come to death.

Rickenbacker served until the end of the war. Afterward, he bought the Indianapolis Motor Speedway and Eastern Airlines. He also flew in special missions during World War II (1939–1945). As in his earlier days, the Ace of Aces remained an adventurer for the rest of his life.

British and German fighter planes over France

3

MARIA BOTCHKAREVA: RUSSIAN PEASANT

By 1917, Russian soldiers were worn out from fighting. Many were fleeing the army. Others refused to obey orders. Meanwhile, many women wanted to play a bigger part in the war. One of these women was Maria Botchkareva, a Russian peasant nicknamed Yashka. She had received special permission to enlist as a soldier in the Russian army. Wounded several times, Yashka fought in terrible battles against German machine-gun fire. Risking her own life, she even dragged other wounded soldiers to safety.

ORGANIZING THE BATTALION

In 1917, Yashka suggested organizing an all-female **battalion**. These women could use their fighting spirit to inspire the men. The Russian government agreed. Yashka named her battalion the Women's Battalion of Death.

Almost 2,000 women signed up. Some were peasants, factory workers, and maids. Others were wealthy ladies or college graduates. Even a princess joined the group. Yashka marched the women into a barbershop to have their hair cropped short. Day after day, Yashka trained them.

"As soon as one of them disobeyed an order I quickly removed her uniform and let her go," Yashka said. She knew her women had to be successful. If not, she would "become the laughingstock of the country." After training, only about 300 women were left.

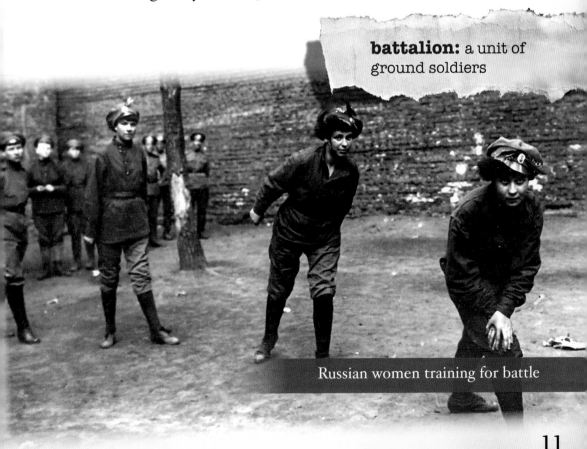

battalion: a unit of ground soldiers

Russian women training for battle

INTO THE TRENCHES

In July 1917, Yashka's group was ordered to the German front in southwestern Russia. Each soldier carried 65 pounds (29 kilograms) of equipment. Their rations consisted of two traditional Russian foods—cabbage soup and a porridge known as kasha. They also had bread, sugar, and tea.

The women headed into the trenches under the light of the moon. Yashka remained determined to succeed. "Don't be cowards! Don't be traitors!" she urged her troops. "I know that you are of the stuff to win glory. The country is watching you set the stride for the entire front."

THE DAY OF BATTLE

Yashka's women lined up in the deep trenches. With their rifles ready, they stood shoulder to shoulder with the men. All through the night, flashes of German cannon fire lit up the horizon. Meanwhile, the men made jokes about the women soldiers. "We gritted our teeth in fury but did not reply," Yashka said.

When the signal was given at last, only the women charged ahead. One woman after another was shot down. But they kept moving forward. Would the men ever join them?

Members of the Women's Battalion of Death

Finally the men swarmed the battlefield. Against a steady hail of gunfire, the Russians overwhelmed the German line. The Germans retreated deep into the forest.

Yashka watched as survivors made their way back to the trenches. Dozens of her troops had been wounded or killed. Still, Yashka's group encouraged many women to fight. New women's battalions were organized all over Russia.

4

KANDE KAMARA: AFRICAN WARRIOR

African soldiers

Kande Kamara was the son of a village chief in French Guinea. At the time, French Guinea was a **colony** of France in West Africa. When war broke out, France began recruiting soldiers from its African colonies. Kamara jumped at the chance to fight. His father had been a warrior, and he wanted to be one too.

INTO THE UNKNOWN

Kamara's army experience was not as exciting as he had expected. Instead, it was disappointing and sad. "We black African soldiers were very sorrowful about the white man's war," he remembered. The Africans went through their training drills, but they weren't told the war's purpose. Kamara said, "There was never any soldier in the camp who knew why we were fighting."

After training, Kamara and his fellow soldiers were sent to Europe. They traveled six days and nights by ship. Many got seasick. Others feared that they would be sold into slavery.

colony: a place that is settled by people from another country and is controlled by that country

"We black African soldiers were very sorrowful about the white man's war."

African soldiers waiting to fight

FIGHTING FROM THE GUTTERS

European-style fighting was confusing for Kamara. The Africans were used to face-to-face combat, but Europeans had different methods of warfare. Warplanes were just one example. Kamara had never even seen an airplane before. And now the sky was filled with these strange war machines. "Steamships ... flew on the air," he said.

Each soldier dug a trench. Kamara called them gutters. He said, "You had to dig your own gutter, no one would do it for you. You were given all the tools in your kit: iron picks on your chest, shovels and the pick-axes tied to your backpack. I tried to dig a small hole to hide my whole body."

Everyone hid in the trenches, waiting for the enemy to show up. On the officer's command, soldiers scrambled out and fired at once. Africans usually fought their enemies one-on-one. But here, they "never really saw the people they killed," Kamara said.

About 212,000 Africans from France's West African colonies fought during the war. About 30,000 of those men died in combat. As for Kamara, he returned home safely after the war.

"You had to dig your own gutter, no one would do it for you."

In the Trenches

Trench warfare was widespread during World War I. Trenches were about 12 feet [4 meters] deep. Hundreds of men dug for hours to make them. Inside the trenches, soldiers were packed shoulder-to-shoulder. Enemy trenches faced each other across a stretch of ground called no-man's-land. Barbed wire stretched in front of each trench to keep enemies away. Going "over the top" meant charging out of the trench, often into a stream of enemy fire. Neither side had good plans for breaking an enemy trench line without suffering heavy losses.

5

ARTHUR EMPEY: AMERICAN SOLDIER IN GREAT BRITAIN

Early in 1917, American Arthur Empey was anxious to go to war. He was angry about German attacks on U.S. submarines. But the United States had not yet entered World War I. Empey didn't want to wait for the United States to join. He sailed to Great Britain and signed up with the British army.

DEADLY GASES

Empey faced scary new weapons on the battlefield. One was poison gas that attacked victims' lungs and skin. Empey saw many soldiers suffer from poison gas attacks. He felt helpless watching a fellow soldier die this way. To wage a gas attack, soldiers usually lined up poison gas cylinders along the trenches. When the wind shifted toward the enemy, the cylinders were opened. Then the gas floated toward its victims. Other times the gas cylinders were fired from large guns toward enemy lines.

THE MAD SCRAMBLE

Empey faced the Germans from a trench in France. At one point, a lookout shouted, "There's a sort of greenish, yellow cloud rolling along the ground out in front, it's coming ..." Empey started banging on an empty artillery shell case. This was the alarm signal for a gas attack.

The soldiers scrambled to put on gas helmets. The cloth hoods had two glass windows to see through. Chemicals in the cloth helped screen out the gas.

"Gas travels quickly, so you must not lose any time," Empey explained. "You generally have about eighteen or twenty seconds." One soldier was not fast enough. He grabbed his throat, dropped to the ground, and died within seconds.

Soldiers fought in clouds of poison gas.

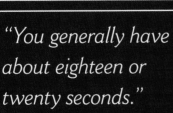

"You generally have about eighteen or twenty seconds."

TAKING A HIT

After the gas attack, German machine-gun and artillery fire began exploding everywhere. Suddenly Empey heard a deafening bang, and his head felt like it was blowing up. A bullet had pierced his gas helmet. Next he noticed his "head began to swim, throat got dry, and a heavy pressure on the lungs ... needles seemed to be pricking flesh, then blackness."

Empey was unconscious for three hours while his company fought back the Germans. When he awoke he helped fellow survivors bury the dead—including Germans. "In death there is not much distinction," Empey said. "Friend and foe are treated alike."

Among the dead was a muddy little dog. Empey's company had kept it in their camp as a pet. He found the dog "lying dead, with his two paws over his nose." Empey noted sadly, "It's the animals that suffer the most."

After the war, Empey wrote about his experiences in the book *Over the Top*. It was a huge success and encouraged many Americans to join the army. The book was later made into a movie with Empey as the star.

Gas masks helped protect soldiers from deadly gas attacks.

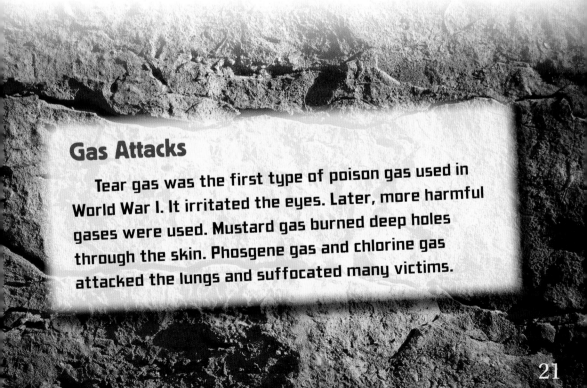

Gas Attacks

Tear gas was the first type of poison gas used in World War I. It irritated the eyes. Later, more harmful gases were used. Mustard gas burned deep holes through the skin. Phosgene gas and chlorine gas attacked the lungs and suffocated many victims.

6 ADOLF VON SPIEGEL: GERMAN U-BOAT COMMANDER

German U-boat

German submarines, called U-boats, were the terror of the seas. Hidden underwater, they fired torpedoes that demolished ships. Adolf K.G.E. von Spiegel knew what it was like to cause this damage. He served on the U-202 and was the commander of the U-32 and U-93.

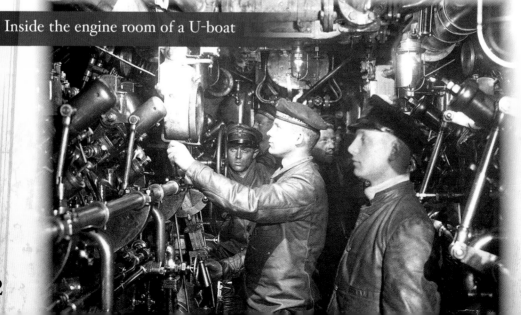
Inside the engine room of a U-boat

READY, AIM, FIRE!

One day von Spiegel spotted a British ship through his periscope. To his surprise, there were rows and rows of horses on deck. Tanks were beginning to replace horseback soldiers. But many horses still carried both warriors and supplies. "Oh heavens, horses! What a pity, those lovely beasts!" von Spiegel thought. But he knew what he had to do. With the ship in his sights, von Spiegel shouted "Fire!" The torpedo sped toward its mark.

A single torpedo hit could demolish a ship.

A HORRIFIC SCENE

The submarine crew broke out in cheers. But a horrific scene was unfolding aboard the ship. Screaming men rushed everywhere. They shoved one another to get to the lifeboats. Horses slipped on the wet decks as they reared up on their hind legs. Both men and horses began jumping overboard. "I saw a beautiful long-tailed dapple-grey horse take a mighty leap," von Spiegel said.

The German commander couldn't stand to watch any longer. He had racked up another torpedo strike. That's all that mattered. He steered the sub into a steep dive and fled to the deep-sea waters below.

Aboard the Ships

Living conditions aboard submarines were miserable. The men lived and worked in damp spaces. Their bunks were so cramped they couldn't even stretch out. The subs were constantly rocking, causing seasickness.

"I saw a beautiful long-tailed dapple-grey horse take a mighty leap."

7 PEACE AT LAST

Newspapers reported the war's end.

One by one, the Central powers collapsed. Finally Germany signed an **armistice** with the Allied powers on November 11, 1918. World War I was over.

armistice: a temporary agreement to stop fighting

Fighters had more in common than they had differences. No nationality, race, or gender was short on bravery. They all shared the thrill of victory and the gloom of defeat. Many fighters showed sympathy for the enemy.

Why did one person live and another die? Sometimes it was just a matter of chance. Often the fighting seemed senseless. As Kande Kamara said, "We just fought and fought until we got exhausted and died."

People around the world celebrated the end of World War I.

In a way, there were no winners in this war. Millions lost their loved ones. Homes and cities were left in ruins. Many people saw these losses as awful but necessary. After all, they believed this was the war to end all wars. They never imagined there would be a second world war.

A military grave site located in France

GLOSSARY

ace (ACE)—someone who has shot down at least five enemy aircraft

Allied powers (AL-lyd PAU-uhrs)—a group of countries that fought the Central powers in World War I; the Allies included the United States, Great Britain, France, Russia, and Italy

altitude (AL-ti-tood)—the height a plane flies above the ground

armistice (ARM-iss-tiss)—a temporary agreement to stop fighting a war

battalion (buh-TAL-yuhn)—a unit of ground soldiers

Central powers (SEN-truhl PAU-uhrs)—a group of countries that fought the Allied powers in World War I; the Central powers included Germany and Austria-Hungary

colony (KAH-luh-nee)—a place that is settled by people from another country and is controlled by that country

peasant (PEZ-uhnt)—a poor farm worker

periscope (PER-uh-skope)—a tube-shaped viewing device; crew members can use a periscope to view the water's surface from a submerged submarine

ration (RASH-uhn)—daily amount of food given to a soldier

recruit (ri-KROOT)—to ask someone to join a company or organization

shrapnel (SHRAP-nuhl)—small pieces of metal scattered by an exploding shell or bomb

squadron (SKWAHD-ruhn)—an official military unit

traitor (TRAY-tuhr)—someone who turns against his or her country

BIBLIOGRAPHY

Botchkareva, Maria. *Yashka: My Life as Peasant, Officer and Exile.* New York: Frederick A. Stokes, 1919.

Empey, Arthur Guy. *Over the Top.* New York: G. P. Putnam's Sons, 1917.

"Gas Attack, 1916." Eyewitness to History. http://www.eyewitnesstohistory.com/gas.htm

Iliffe, John. *Honour in African History.* New York: Cambridge University Press, 2005.

Rickenbacker, Edward V. *Fighting the Flying Circus.* New York: Frederick A. Stokes Company, 1919.

"U-boat Attack, 1916." Eyewitness to History. http://www.eyewitnesstohistory.com/sub.htm

READ MORE

Adams, Simon. *World War I*. DK Eyewitness Books. New York: DK Publishing, 2007.

Hibbert, Adam. *In the Trenches in WWI*. On the Front Line. Chicago: Raintree, 2006.

Worth, Richard. *America in World War I*. Wars that Changed American History. Milwaukee: World Almanac Library, 2007.

INTERNET SITES

FactHound offers a safe, fun way to find Internet sites related to this book. All of the sites on FactHound have been researched by our staff.

Here's all you do:

Visit *www.facthound.com*

Type in this code: 9781429647373

INDEX